Monarch Migration: Counting by 10s

by Megan Atwood

illustrated by Sharon Holm

Content Consultant: Paula J. Maida, PhD

magic wagon

VISIT US AT
WWW.ABDOPUBLISHING.COM

Published by Magic Wagon, a division of the ABDO Group, PO Box 398166, Minneapolis, MN 55439. Copyright © 2012 by Abdo Consulting Group, Inc. International copyrights reserved in all countries. All rights reserved. No part of this book may be reproduced in any form without written permission from the publisher.

Looking Glass Library™ is a trademark and logo of Magic Wagon.

Printed in the United States of America, North Mankato, Minnesota.
102011
012012

 THIS BOOK CONTAINS AT LEAST 10% RECYCLED MATERIALS.

Text by Megan Atwood
Illustrations by Sharon Holm
Edited by Lisa Owings
Interior layout by Kazuko Collins
Cover design by Christa Schneider

Library of Congress Cataloging-in-Publication Data

Atwood, Megan.
  Monarch migration : counting by 10s / by Megan Atwood ; illustrated by Sharon Lane Holm.
      p. cm. — (Count the critters)
   ISBN 978-1-61641-854-0
1. Counting—Juvenile literature. 2. Set theory—Juvenile literature. I. Holm, Sharon Lane, ill. II. Title.
   QA113.A895 2012
   513.2'11—dc23
                              2011033076

You can count faster when counting by tens. Let's count by tens while these monarch butterflies get ready to fly south. Monarchs fly south in the fall because winter is cold. To count them by tens, add ten to the last number you counted.

Monarchs flit and flutter. Ten monarchs flit into the woods. They open and close their orange and black wings.

10   **20**   **30**   **40**   **50**   **60**

Count the monarchs slowly:
one, two, three, four, five, six,
seven, eight, nine, ten.

0 + 10 = 10

10 **20** **30** **40** **50** **60**

Monarchs flutter and flit. Ten more monarchs flutter into the woods to join their friends. Monarch wings are covered in tiny scales. Count the monarchs quickly by tens: ten, twenty.

70   80   90   100   10+10=20

10   20   30   40   50   60

Monarchs sip and slurp. Ten more monarchs fly into the woods. They use their antennae to find the flowers with the sweetest nectar to sip. Count the monarchs by tens: ten, twenty, thirty.

70 80 90 100 20+10=30

Monarchs slurp and sip. Ten more monarchs look for food. They slurp nectar from flowers. A butterfly mouth is called a proboscis. Count the monarchs by tens: ten, twenty, thirty, forty.

10   20   30   40   50   60

70   80   90   100   30+10=40

Monarchs float and fly. More
monarchs float on the breeze
and land in the trees. They are
glad to join their butterfly friends.

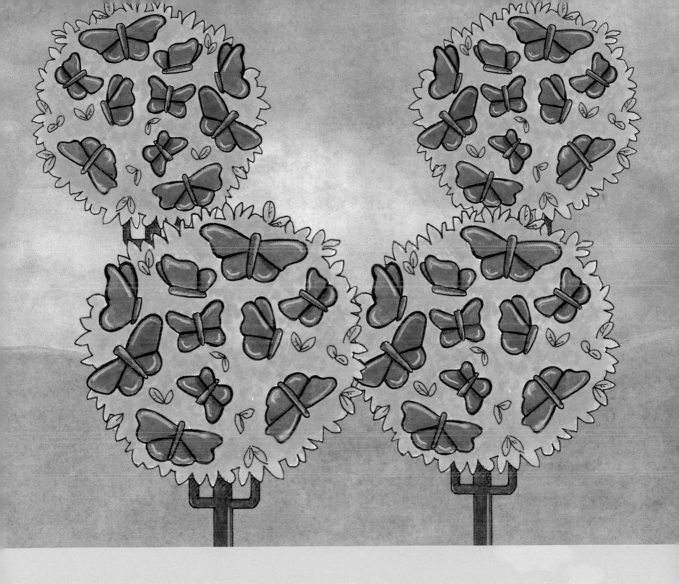

Count the monarchs by tens:

ten, twenty, thirty, forty, fifty.

70   80   90   100   40+10=50

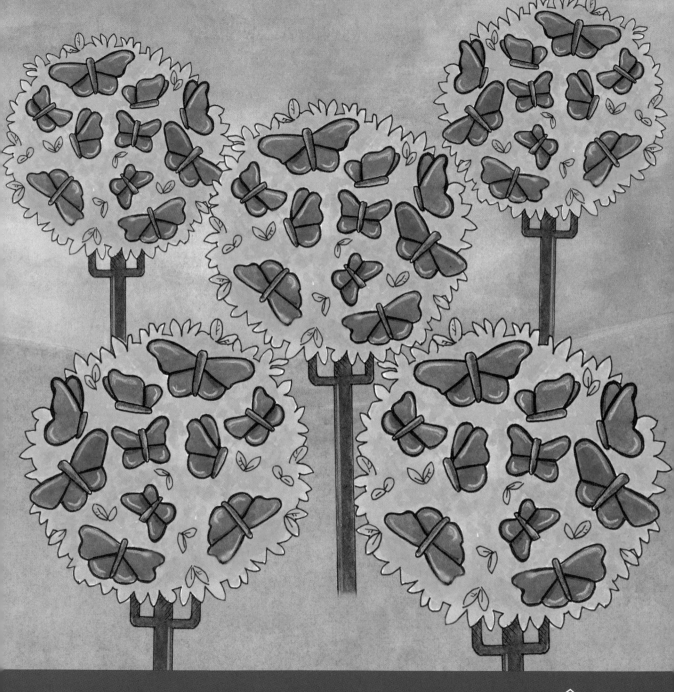

10   20   30   40   50   60

Monarchs fly and float. Still more monarchs fly into the woods. They spread their wings to ride on the wind. Count the monarchs by tens: ten, twenty, thirty, forty, fifty, sixty.

70   80   90   100   50+10=60

Monarchs rest and relax. Ten tired monarchs have flown a long way. They have come to the woods to find branches to rest on. Count the monarchs by tens: ten, twenty, thirty, forty, fifty, sixty, seventy.

10   20   30   40   50   60

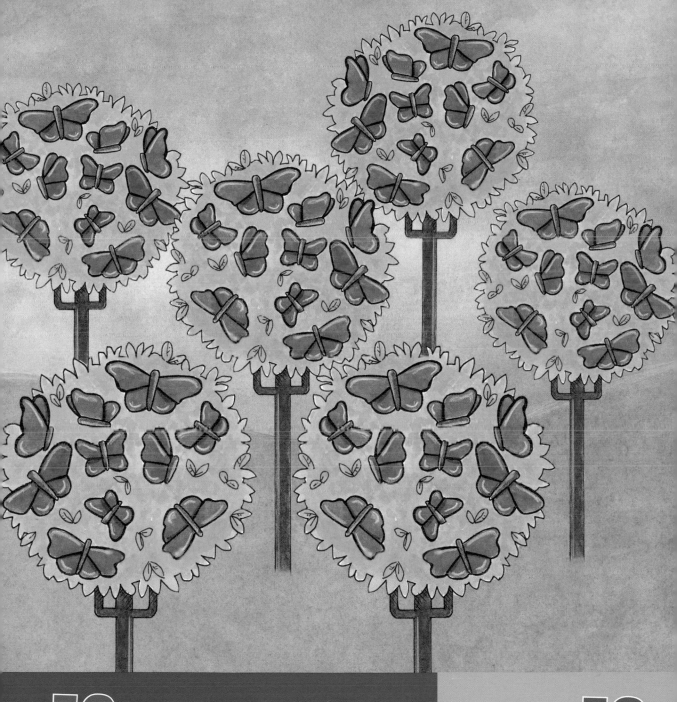

70　80　90　100　60+10=70

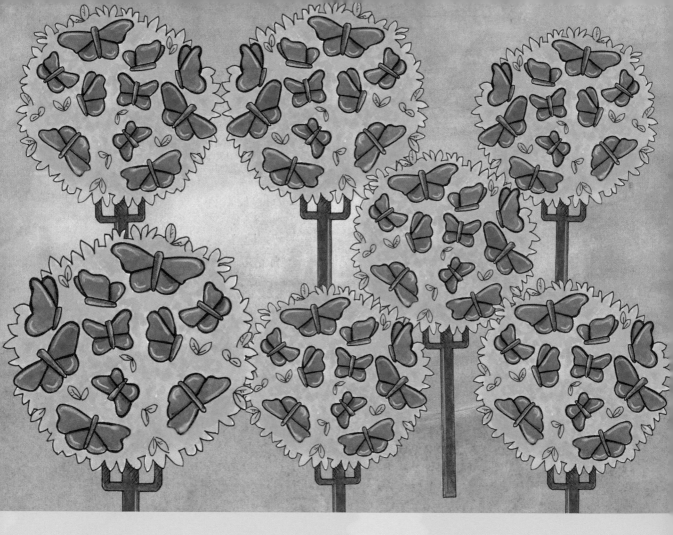

Monarchs relax and rest. Ten more monarchs find a tree and relax. They close their bright wings after they land.

10   20   30   40   50   60

Count the monarchs by tens: ten, twenty, thirty, forty, fifty, sixty, seventy, eighty.

70 80 90 100 70+10=80

Monarchs rest and relax. Ten more monarchs fly into the woods to join their friends. It's almost time to go! Count the monarchs by tens: ten, twenty, thirty, forty, fifty, sixty, seventy, eighty, ninety.

10   20   30   40   50   60

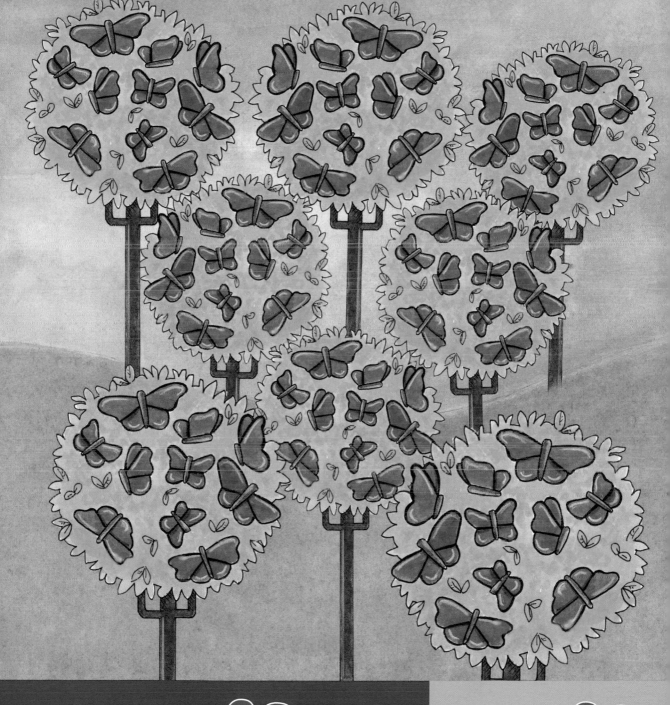

70   80   90   100   80+10=90

The last ten monarchs are finally here. All the monarchs lift their wings and fly into the air together. Count them by tens: ten, twenty, thirty, forty, fifty, sixty, seventy, eighty, ninety, one hundred monarchs! Time to go south!

10   20   30   40   50   60

70   80   90   100   90+10=100

Words to Know

antennae—feelers on top of butterfly heads; butterflies smell with their antennae.

flit—to move quickly from one place to another.

flutter—to flap the wings quickly.

monarch butterfly—a type of butterfly with orange and black wings.

nectar—a sweet liquid from flowers that butterflies feed on.

proboscis—the straw-shaped mouth of a butterfly.

scale—a small, thin plate like a fish scale.

Web Sites

To learn more about counting by 10s, visit ABDO Group online at **www.abdopublishing.com**. Web sites about counting are featured on our Book Links page. These links are routinely monitored and updated to provide the most current information available.

10 20 30 40 50 60 70 80 90 100